The Ripple Effect

A Book About Mastery

The Ripple Effect

A Book About Mastery

Written with Love, Peace, and Gratitude

by:
**Dr. Thomas Edward Gargiula
(Dr. G.)**

Copyright © 2009 – Dr. Thomas Edward Gargiula

All rights reserved. No part of this book may be used or reproduced in any manner whatsoever without written permission from the publisher, except in the case of brief quotations embodied in critical articles and reviews.

This material has been written and published solely for educational purposes. The author and the publisher shall have neither liability nor responsibility to any person or entity with respect to any loss, damage or injury caused or alleged to be caused directly or indirectly by the information contained in the book.

Third Edition
10 9 8 7 6 5 4

Interior Design by Rudy Milanovich & Keith Leon

Contact Dr. G. at: DrG@TheRippleEffectLife.com

For additional copies:
www.lulu.com/TheRippleEffect

All Rights Reserved
Life Development Technologies

Table of Contents

Endorsements..7
Acknowledgements..9
Introduction..11

Chapter 1: Thoughts - The Law of Attraction...............15

Chapter 2: Where is God in All of This? 31

Chapter 3: Taking Responsibility For Your Life...........35

Chapter 4: Change Can Be Difficult.............................43

Chapter 5: How We Impact Others' Lives....................49

Chapter 6: The Keys to Living An Inspired Life..........57

Chapter 7: Growth is a Process.....................................63

Chapter 8: Drawing A Line In The Sand 71

Chapter 9: Who Cares What Other People Think.........75

Chapter 10: Upgrading The Quality of Your Life...........81

Chapter 11: Knowing That You Are Creating / Living Your I.D.E.A.L. Life...89

Chapter 12: Working On BEING Instead Of DOING....93

Chapter 13: The Ripple Effect of Time Mastery 117

Conclusion: There Is No Them - There Is Only US......125

Endorsements

"Dr. G totally gets it. Consciously creating your life is what it is all about. *The Ripple Effect* shows you the formula, the motivation, and the fun in creating the life you want to live. Pick up a copy for you and someone you care about today!"

— Keith Leon
Book mentor and author of the bestselling book,
Who Do You Think You Are?
Discover The Purpose Of Your Life

"You never know how far reaching something you may read today will affect your life and the lives of those you love so profoundly tomorrow...and for the rest of their lives. You're holding in your hands a book that provokes positive thought and lifestyle change in your life, your future and the way you embrace your world!"

— Dr. Steve Hoffman
Speaker - Author - Educator
Discover Wellness, Inc. and
2nd Cousin Media/Marketing

"Dr. G has done an excellent job of bringing numerous spiritual matters down to a practical realm of application. His book, *The Ripple Effect,* and he, as a living example, have enlightened me on the sources of my stress. Through the ideas and activities suggested in his book, I realized living a life congruent with my heart and purpose, dispelled the "in-congruent" stressors that needn't exist in my life in the first place."

— Steve Herbst
Air Operations Officer for Headquarters Air Mobility
Command, Scott Air Force Base

Acknowledgment

My wife, Sue, has been such a pure sense of inspiration and support over the years and in the creation of this book. Thank you honey – I Love You with all of my heart.

Our children Nick, Matt, Maria and Natalie are my greatest teachers about the laws of life. They are truly God's biggest gift to us.

Jeff Smith, Steve Hoffman, Patrick Gentempo, Chris Kent, Tony Palermo, David Jackson, Tom Preston, Keith Leon, Wayne Dyer, Dan Millman, John Demartini and Mark Victor Hansen are just a few of the mentors, teachers and coaches that have directly molded the content of this work.

Lennie Appelquist and Elizabeth LaPrade have been integral in the creation of this books supporting website.

My parents, Ed and Fran, laid the foundation that allows me to have the impact that my life is having upon this world.

My Brother, Rich, has been one of my biggest cheerleaders in all that I do – Thank you for always believing in me.

Finally, I thank Jesus Christ for being my Lord and Savior. I thank Jesus Christ for blessing me in so many ways. I am grateful for the vision in the creation of this work and for the impact that it will have upon His world.

Introduction (A Must Read)

My Life Purpose is: To bring peace, prosperity and enlightenment to the world by helping people to consciously create their life in their own I.D.E.A.L. – By identifying and striving to eliminate contradictions in their life.

I.D.E.A.L.:

- I : To live a life that has positive IMPACT
- D: To live with DIVINITY
- E: To live life EFFORTLESSLY
- A: To be ATTRACTIVE – Love Yourself
- L: To Always come from a position of LOVE

The name "The Ripple Effect" came to me as the perfect title of this work because of the visual image it portrays when you hear the words. Picture a pond that is perfectly calm. It is so smooth that it looks like glass. See yourself throwing a stone into the middle of that pond. What do you see? ... YES – a Ripple that seems to go on forever. It seems to flow out so far that it touches all parts of the pond. Not one square inch of the pond's surface is left unaffected by the Ripple. The entire pond has been impacted and touched by the action of that one stone.

The pond is the world and the stone is each and every action you chose to take in your life. Even the actions that seem little and insignificant are a stone as well. They are ALL accounted for. They ALL make a difference.

The title says that this is a book about Mastery. What will mastering your life do for you? Well – life will certainly be more enjoyable and fulfilling – but it is not only about what your Life Mastery will do for you – it is about what it will do as your *mastery* Ripples out and impacts the rest of the world. Your life is already extremely significant; through Mastery you will be able to assist others in raising up their lives and allow them to have a bigger impact upon this world.

It is important to understand the extreme magnitude of responsibility that comes with this knowledge.

Your life is God's gift to you and what you choose to do with your life is your gift back to God.

How we live each day is our responsibility. Nobody else is responsible for our choices in life. In our society today many people pass when it comes to responsibility. They even pass on the responsibility for their own health, wealth, child rearing, jobs, morals, ethics, standards, and values. This is a simple fact and truth, all of these items, and many more, are 100% our individual responsibility.

The "Ripple Effect" is the result of how your life and actions will extend out and affect the lives of millions of people.

To understand the power of "The Ripple Effect" we will discuss several truths about Life, God, and Natural Law. "The Ripple Effect" (how your life affects other people) is the result of your *actions*. Your *actions* are the result of your Feelings. Your Feelings are a direct result of your Thoughts.

So, let's begin with your Thoughts…

Chapter One

Thoughts: The Law of Attraction

"What you think about and focus upon, expands!!!"

What we choose to think about controls our life. When we think about good things we tend to attract good things into our life. When we think about abundance we attract abundance as well. The paradox with this simple truth is that when we think about negative things and negative situations we attract those too. It is The Law of Attraction, it is simple and it works.

It is very important that you become aware of The Law of Attraction. You must realize that it does work, understand how it works and then, how to use it to your advantage.

The first rule to be aware of is "Talk to yourself with the utmost respect, love and peace." Our self-talk determines how our mind thinks. When we speak positively to ourselves we have positive thoughts and when we speak negatively to ourselves we have negative thoughts. I know it sounds very simple. You are right!!! Many things in life are very simple and very powerful – and often times overlooked. How we think is so simple that we often forget how powerful it is. Our thought process may have been programmed by our upbringing. However, *this is simply a fact* and *not an excuse*. Remember, our thoughts are *our* responsibility. Let us get up and take a stand here. Decide right now that you want to consciously create your own life. Realize how good that feels and how freeing it is.

Here are three simple ways to guarantee that you will be thinking positive thoughts:

1. The Gratitude Principle
2. Positive Affirmations
3. Staying in the present moment

The Gratitude Principle

Take time each day to look for things to be grateful and thankful for. You should not have to look too far. This is actually a fun game we can play. What this game does for us is gently nudge us to focus on the positive. Begin right now. Stop reading for a minute and think of something for which you are grateful…

Dr. Thomas Edward Gargiula

Write it down:

_____

_____

_____

_____

_____

_____

_____

_____

_____

_____

_____

_____

_____

Excellent!

Do not go on until you have written your list. After starting your list, read the following examples and then add more to your current list. Making the list is part of the *actions* that I was talking about. If you do not do the *actions*, nothing will change in your life.

Here are some examples of what we can be thankful for and how to word them in a positive way.

"Thank you for my health!"
"Thank you for my abundance!"

Even if we have debt, find where you have abundance in your life and be thankful for that abundance. Be thankful for the $5 in your pocket. Be thankful for the loose change in a jar or in your drawer. Be thankful for the job that you do have.

"Thank you for my family!"
"Thank you for my friends!"
"Thank you for my freedoms!"
"Thank you for my gifts and abilities!"
"Thank you for the fact that I can read these words!"

You get the idea. It is simple…but it is NOT easy.

It does take practice. It takes **Kaisen**.

Kaisen is a Japanese principle that says - true progress takes constant and never-ending improvement.

When you look at it, most people who have achieved any level of success in any area of their life have done so over a period of time... *learning* and *improving* along the journey.

The idea is not to be perfect, but to be better today than you were last week and better *next* week than you are today - And for each week thereafter. Keep being aware of your thoughts, and keep striving to improve them.

Positive Affirmations

Affirmations are statements that you write down so you can read them each day. Positive affirmations are positive statements about your life as it is now and as you see it changing and progressing. They are not wishes and whims. They are meaningful and very, very real.

Here are some examples of positive affirmations:

"I see the genius in everyone I meet today."
"I am a person loaded with great gifts and abilities."
"I love to give and I love to share."
"Wonderful opportunities are seeking me because I am ready for great success in my life."
"I love me!!!"
"I am worthy of being loved by everyone."
"I enjoy sharing love and bringing peace to every place I go today."

Again…it is simple, but *not* easy. Set thirty minutes aside in the next 24 hours to write down a list of at least twenty positive affirmations. Read and expand this list daily until it reaches fifty affirmations over the next thirty days. Commit to this simple act and see how your life begins to change. You will see the direction of your life begin to shift as you shift the way your mind works. What you begin to focus on will become attracted into your life.

Eventually you will not need a list. Your thoughts will become automatic and always lean in the positive direction. Be sure to not discount the extreme power of such a simple task. If you choose to shortcut the system your results will be less than what you are wanting in your life. You are worth it, so take every important step along the way.

Positive Affirmations:

_____

_____

_____

_____

_____

_____

_____

Dr. Thomas Edward Gargiula

Staying In The Present Moment

The past is where guilt lies; the future is where fear lives, God's abundance lives only in the present. How many times in your day do you find yourself thinking about what has already happened? Most of the time those thoughts are about what you did not like and how you wish it went differently. If we are not thinking about the past, we are focusing on what we think is going to happen at some point in the future. – This is Chatter.

Have a mind with no chatter…no noise…and no judgments. That is very easy to say, but WOW, it is sure challenging to do. Let us break apart the previous statement and study it.

Have a mind with no chatter

What does that mean? Let's think about this for a minute. Our mind is frequently speaking, thinking, commenting, and formulating a response. This chatter can get very noisy. We often do not hear what a person is really saying to us. We are too busy formulating our response.

A step that can help all of us is to really listen to our minds to see how much chatter is really going on. Focus on your mind and visualize yourself turning down the volume. This can be done by doing whatever it is you do that will relax your mind.

Prayer
Meditation
Visualization
Yoga

As we quiet our mind, we begin to finally hear with new ears. This can take a lot of practice. However – it is worth every second of practice. It is truly something to be mastered. It can be mastered by anyone. It simply takes time, practice and focus.

This is a very important exercise because most of what our mind is chattering about is what happened in the past or what we are worrying or fearful about happening in the future.

Let us think about some simple facts;

The past is only something we should *learn* from.

There is *nothing* in the past that we can change.

Our level of guilt and regret *will not* influence what happened in the past.

If we do not learn from past mistakes, then those mistakes were wasted and they will surely be repeated.

The beauty and the purpose of mistakes is that *each problem* (mistake) has within it an inherent answer – and lesson - that is greater than the problem itself.

.

Once you find the lesson, recognize its beauty and are thankful for its existence in your life – then and only then does the mistake become a true gift.

Now you must forgive yourself and anyone else who needs your forgiveness in order for you to have closure with any past issues.

If you are unwilling to forgive, unwilling to learn the lessons and move on with your life, you should stop reading now and come back when you are ready to forgive. This step is that important. Sometimes the hardest person to forgive is you. If you choose to not forgive, you are stalling your life by being in defense mode. It is impossible for your body or your life to be in defense mode and growth mode at the same time. You must choose one. By not forgiving, you are automatically choosing defense mode. This defense mode will permeate every aspect of your life. Your health, your growth, your spirit, your finances, your relationships, and your ability to serve and give back. WOW – by choosing this for your life you are choosing to do nothing with this great gift that you have been so blessed by GOD to receive.

Life mastery, true health, and wellness will not be achieved until the step of *forgiveness* can be accomplished.

I have been working with people for over 18 years who have health issues and concerns that are keeping them from living life the way they want. My own experience combined with years of research by numerous scientists shows that over 85% of people's health concerns are related to an overwhelming feeling of stress in their lives. If this stress is not dealt with, we will never truly heal. The body will not heal because when we are unable to adapt to stress we create Subluxations in our body. These Subluxations are areas of Nerve Interference. Nerve Interference leads to a loss of function, "dis-ease", and then a low quality of life. As a Chiropractor my job is to locate and correct these areas of Subluxation. However, another important part of my job is why I am writing this book. My goal is to share information that will help you to decrease your negative stress. With lowered negative stress it is easy for adaptability to take place. A Subluxation interferes with the incredible expression of health that each of you have within you. If we can decrease the negative stress and increase our adaptability to stress (by removing subluxations) then our expression of health automatically increases and improves.

Two things must happen.

First... you must recognize which area of your life is causing overwhelming stress, and then learn ways to decrease the stress that we would like to lessen. The reason why I say, "to decrease the stress you want to decrease" is because there are many people that do not want to give up certain stresses from their lives.

Some people love the job they have, even though it causes stress.

Athletes frequently choose to do the sports that cause them extreme physical stress.

Others may not like their stress or not want their stress but truly cannot do anything about it. Certain things in life happen and we cannot directly do anything about them. Such as:

> The death of a loved one
> The loss of a job
> A Natural Disaster

But wait; there *is* something you can do, even about difficult situations. You get to choose how you are going to react or respond to them. You can take the loss of a job or a Natural Disaster as the perfect opportunity to reinvent yourself. This is when you could sit back and ask yourself, "What do I really, really, really want?, Where do I really want to live?, and what do I really want to do for a 'living'?"

The more challenging event to understand is the loss of a loved one, especially when it is a child. From the world's perspective, death is hard to understand. From a spiritual perspective it is part of the program. We all hope to live a long healthy life, doing good, being a positive influence, and raising beautiful children who take your accomplishments and further them all the more. Then we all leave this world at a ripe old age. It sounds good, but it does not always happen that way. Even these difficult situations can be responded to in many different ways. One common response is to blame God and to think that

God made a mistake. I do not mean to oversimplify this response, but the more we respond with unconditional love and faith in and for God, the easier it will be to see God's plan and to embrace life.

This is one reason why you must live in the present. When you live in the past and in the future you waste today. You do not see it and use it for the gift that it is. Even the death of a child or the death of someone in the prime of their life has a purpose. Think about it this way. No one ever questions when someone is born. Yet we always question when someone leaves this world. If someone does not live as long as we think they should, we say it is a tragedy. Who are we to say how long one person lives as compared to another? It also has nothing to do with how much we have accomplished or have left to do in this world. Be grateful for everyday and enjoy each moment of everyday and we will live with no regrets. It is typically the things left unsaid and undone that cause us sadness when someone dies. These same things cause us to have regret in our own lives.

Second… we must adapt to the stresses that we cannot decrease and to the stresses that we *choose* not to decrease.

Adapting or not adapting to stress is like the difference between a new green branch and an old dry one. The green one can be bent in all kinds of directions and will be just fine. The old dry one will crack, break and be permanently damaged. The same goes for us. When we adapt, we go with the flow. When we do not adapt we break! When I say adapt and go with the flow, I am referring to the 95% of the things we worry about that really are insignificant or totally out of our control.

Think about it, why spend sleepless nights worrying if it is going to rain on your wedding day. You have NO CONTROL over this. Put your mind at ease by having a backup plan if it does rain and forget about it.

For the 5% of things that are in our control and are truly meaningful to us and important to our values, then consciously choose to take on those stresses. Be happy and grateful that you have the freedom and ability to do so.

A living example of this is how Senior Citizens respond to life. Since they have more life experience they tend to be more relaxed and laid back about what *used* to stress them out and what currently stresses us out. I have said on many occasions that the parents I have *now* are not the same parents that I grew up with. They see my children, their actions, energy and playful nature as cute and funny. When I was my children's age and I did the same thing or asked the same questions I did not always get the same happy and positive response from the same people. I am being very respectful when I speak about my parents. I have seen a change in my parents and I am very happy to see this change. I am happy for them. They seem to have more life enjoyment and are able to really appreciate the blessing of their grandchildren.

The lesson from our parents is to learn how to respond

the way they do. We should do this now, Instead of waiting until we are grandparents.

My parents are not unique to this scenario. I have observed this same thing in hundreds of other people as well.

What allows for this change to occur? Their life experience puts things into a different perspective. Once you have raised your children you realize in hindsight what is serious and important and what is not serious and unimportant.

The other aspect about life that they have seemed to learn is a healthy selfishness. This means to give out of *your abundance*. Having so much love of *self* that it spills over to everyone else you meet each day. The same goes for time, money, peace and compassion. How useful are you as a parent when you are tired, stressed out and frazzled. Not too useful. Take care of you. Women are much worse about this than men. Set time aside for you. Treat yourself. Pamper yourself. Love yourself. The only way to do any of these things is by shifting your thinking. Many of you are thinking – Yeah it sounds good but there is NO time for me. Remember – what you think about expands. If you are thinking that there is no time you will get more "No Time". Things will happen and come up to swallow the opportunities to take time for yourself.

First, know that you are worth the time.
Second, honor your time and others will too.

Notes

Chapter Two

Where is God in all of this?

"In the beginning was the Word,
And the Word was with God,
And the Word was God." – John 1:1

God seems to have a plan for us. He wants us to *Love One Another*. We do this as a result of how we serve one another. This service will have an impact on the people of this world. However, we are blessed with free will. We get to choose! We either listen to God or listen to the busyness of society, politics and gossip. The latter is supported by the media, especially Television. The great thing is that at any point in our life if we choose to stop listening to the world and begin to listen to God, He will be there for us. He is everywhere and He is always.

You see, God is always there – waiting. When we choose to show up and decide to put God as the head of our spiritual life, personal life and professional life – then everything takes on a whole new meaning. The conversation goes like this:

> "Thank you God for all the wonderful things You have blessed me with in my life. Even those things that did not seem like blessings at the time. I realize (when looking back) they were necessary, good and perfect for me in order to get to where I am right now."

> "I see all of the positive circumstances, people and events in my life. I am aware and grateful for all the abundances and blessings You have given to me."

> "God, I put You as the head of my life... What can I do to serve You?"

The more we stay connected with God – the clearer the message becomes. We must communicate with God and have a real relationship with Him. Through prayer, meditation, reading His word and through the Holy Eucharist we get closer to God. The closer we get, the more God's plan and our plan begin looking the same.

What a BLESSING!
And what a RESPONSIBILITY!

WOW – that is so powerful because we are living by natural and spiritual laws.

Notes

Notes

Chapter Three

Taking Responsibility For Your Life

"Contradiction leads to destruction!"
– Dr. Patrick Gentempo

This is NOT designed to be a warm and fuzzy "feel good" book. It is being created to potentially change your life... Forever!!!

Why potentially? Well, it is only You who can truly change your life. Not me or anyone else. This is your show; you are the one writing the script and accepting your path. Your decisions create your day-to-day life. Let us become aware and recognize that this is an incredible gift from God. We can create a life that serves the world and God in a grand and wonderful way!!! The more in tune we are with Our True Purpose the closer our life and path comes to what God has designed for us.

It is not a question of IF you are going to have an impact on the world… it is a matter of being aware of the fact that you ARE having an impact on the world.

Everybody's Life IS Significant!

Significant does not have to mean world famous. You do not have to become a household name, like "Oprah", in order to live a life of significance. For those of you who have children in your lives your impact upon them are tremendous. Whether you have children of your own or you are a teacher, coach, priest, doctor, youth leader, neighbor, etc. you have an important role to play. Their lives, minds, thoughts, hearts and futures are molded, advanced and enlightened by the adult role models in their lives. You *are* that role model!!!

An important emotional healing would be to take the frustrations and disappointments from your childhood and pass on the positive messages and actions that would have brought you to a happier and more fulfilled place in life.

Whoa!!! – What was that? Did I say to come to grips with your past?

YES – As it was mentioned earlier. Find the lesson in our past and take the great message of the lesson and bring that to our present and future.

Turn the fact that your dad never spent time with you and make sure you have planned quality time with the children in your life.

Change the negative thoughts you grew up with, about never being good enough and about failure, into positive thoughts, motivation and actions.

Our daughter, Maria, when she was three years old had a set of Monkey Bars at her pre-school. It was her goal to get across all the monkey bars without stopping or falling. After each day at pre-school Maria would report to us how she did. There was never disappointment in her voice. Even on the day when she only got to one bar. One day it would be 3 bars, the next day 5 then 4 and so on. Each time she reported her progress she positively stated that she is getting closer and closer. This great attitude comes from her mother, Sue, and me who always speak with our children from the perspective of being positive about everything. We believe there is good in everything if we look from the right perspective. Finally, one day towards the end of the school year, Maria told me on the phone, as I drove home from my Chiropractic Office (Windmill Family Wellness Center), that she had a surprise for me. As my car pulled into the driveway she rushed out to tell me the surprise. She said she made it across all six monkey bars and she was so proud of herself. I shared with her that I was certainly proud of her as well. I told Maria that I was most proud that she set a goal and practiced and practiced without getting discouraged until she finally reached her goal.

I learn so much from my children each and every day. I think this is why God blessed us with four beautiful children. I have lots of lessons to learn. My life is filled with constant learning experiences. I have learned to look forward to learning experiences and enjoy them because I know that each one brings me to a higher level of wisdom and consciousness.

Look at all "problems" or situations that are not "perfect" in your mind and look for the opportunity inside. Every "problem" has in it the seed of an opportunity that is far greater than the "problem" ever could have been.

If you think you led a sheltered life, take that sheltered life of never being able to make a decision for yourself and change it into a safe environment for a child to make decisions that will be positive for him or her. This process will mold a young mind into one that has the confidence and self-respect to make good decisions in the future. All leaders are decisive. When we raise children to depend upon someone else's opinion we create a life that is limited and in a very small box. Breaking out of that box will be a life long struggle. Teach the children how to make good decisions and you are arming them with a great skill and ability. More importantly, you are blessing them with a life of limitless possibility.

Now we get to play with our decision-making skills

> Many people want to go through life simply getting by, minding their own business and not interfering with what others do or say and how they act. The truth is we are ALL created from the same source. Everything we do or

do not do affects others whether we are aware of it or not. We are ALL interconnected in our thoughts, desires, actions and in-actions.

Opting out is NOT an option. We all have an impact. Since opting out of having an impact is not possible we get to choose.

The choice becomes… how powerful do you want that impact to be?

You can make a great and positive impact or a horrible and ineffective impact… the choice is yours.

Yes, this IS about you taking FULL responsibility for your life. This is what serving God, by serving His people, is all about. It is answering the hard questions. It is about changing things that need to be changed. It is NOT about wondering when someone else is going to change what is "wrong" in this world.

> Most of us have heard the great statement that "Life is God's gift to us, and what we do with that life is our gift to God."
>
> This is one of those statements that whether we believe in it or not - *it is still true.*

**This is designed to be a major wakeup call…
for ALL of us!!!**

We must remember that the life we are presently living is of our own creation. It is the result of all our thoughts, actions and in-actions up to this point in our life. The dominant thoughts in our mind are what attract our relationships, our opportunities, our financial state and our level of Health. It is imperative that we recognize the severity of the impact this has upon our lives. This simple fact alone should dramatically raise your awareness of the responsibility you have to your life from this point on. And for some, this thought scares you quite deeply. Either way it is still true. Your life is a mirror of what you have been focusing on, thinking about and taking action with.

If you don't like the life you are living, change it.

Only you have the power to do so!!!

Visualize it differently!

Our son, Nick, uses visualization when it comes to sports. He started when he was nine years old. It did not matter whether it was soccer, golf, volleyball or baseball. First, he would always mentally see what he wanted to have happen. The result would almost always be what he envisioned. He learned this technique from conversations Sue and I had with him and all our children over the years. It is easy for a child to fall into a negative pattern, especially if we speak to them in a negative tone. I do not mean that we should not correct or discipline our children. We definitely believe in setting boundaries. But we also use positive words when correcting them. Instead of focusing on the negative by saying "stop that" or "do not do that" we focus on a positive action.

Let me give some example of how this works. If our youngest, Natalie, is climbing on the couch, instead of "Stop climbing on the couch" or "get off of the couch" or "No, I told you not to climb on the couch" we will say, "Natalie, please come off of the couch and play over here with puzzles" or "Please come over here and let Mommy read a book with you" or "Natalie, come down here and help Daddy with putting the water bottles in the fridge" or " Let's go outside so Daddy can push you on the swing"

Notes

Notes

Chapter Four

Change can be difficult

"The One thing constant in life is Change"

Q: What can make change easier?

A: Being aware of your Purpose!

The strength to make this change comes from how big your purpose is. The bigness of your purpose comes from how well you are listening to God. Hearing God clearly comes from a deep relationship with God. A deep relationship with God, like any good relationship, is based upon frequent communication. This communication cannot be chance meetings. They should be planned, deliberate and on purpose. These meetings are so important that nothing should get in their way. They are of the highest priority.

Any relationship that is important to you should be an "on purpose" relationship. Something to be worked at, enjoyed, savored and cherished.

Change is good.
Change is inevitable in growth.
Change is powerful.

How do we impact others?

We first impact others by the example of our own life. It is not what we say that impacts people the most, it is our actions that tell the real tale. Anyone can tell you about being honest and good, but if their actions are dishonest and bad their words are hollow and meaningless.

So, what we do and how we live IS the key.

Life is about living and living is a verb. It is all about action. True inactivity equates with death. Since we are alive let's actually LIVE our lives and to their fullest.

Let us take the first action step...Make two lists.

First List – Positive Actions I Currently Take:

_____

_____

_____

_____

_____

_____

_____

Second List – Negative Actions I Currently Take:

_____

_____

_____

_____

_____

_____

_____

It is very important that we are completely honest when we do these types of exercises. If we cannot be honest with a simple list, it is a reflection of what goes on in our daily life. Honesty and Integrity are essential for us to be creating the life of our dreams.

When you look at all of humanity, who are the happiest people out there? It does not matter what language is spoken, the color of the skin or whether they live in a democracy or a dictatorship. Babies of all kinds are the happiest beings in this world.

So let's look at how a baby sees life.

They are all about Love.

This is why we can be having a "bad" day and then see a beautiful baby and we unconsciously break into a wonderful smile. People do this same thing with puppies as well. Babies, of all kinds, only know how to exude love. This is their life and their function. Anything other than love is a learned behavior or response.

Their love goes hand in hand with trust...

They are miniature images of God.

A religious leader was asked, "What is the difference between the Saints and everyone else?" The answer is simple and very profound. The religious leader said, "Saints have Unconditional Love inside of them just like you and me… but they have NOTHING ELSE inside – Only Unconditional Love"

WOW!!!

Think about that for a minute. Every time I think of that line it makes me realize how much "other stuff" most of us have inside. Sometimes there is so much "other stuff" that the Unconditional Love gets buried.

However, it is still in there. The more focused we are on our Purpose the more the "Other Stuff" melts away.

Natalie, our 2 year old, is amazing about how she simply is the personification of God in a little human body. She is nothing but love. Always happy and smiling. So much so that it becomes wonderfully contagious. Wherever she goes she makes people smile. They cannot help but be caught up in her energy of love.

She shows me daily how much more fun life is when we are happy – purposefully happy. Many people let their moods be dictated by circumstance. Think about it. So many times people are happy or sad because of what has happened to them that day. Why not consciously decide that today is going to be a great day regardless of what happens in the course of our day.

Let's continue with the topic of
How Our Life Impacts Others

Notes

Chapter Five

How we impact other's lives!

"Free will is a blessing... with it, comes 100% Responsibility." - Dr. G

We impact others by the choices we make.

By our decisions
Perhaps, when you were young, you were never taught how to make good decisions. This is not an excuse, but it may be a fact. The only way to make a decision is to make a decision. With each decision we make, no matter how small, we improve our ability to make them.

By our standards
Whether high or low, our standards will have an impact upon other people. Think about it, drug dealers impact many young people's lives. They fool them to think their life is wonderful and a ticket out of their current situation. Those of us with high standards have a

responsibility to be so strong that our positive impact outweighs that of those who have low standards. An important thing to note along this thought process is that we are no better than those who have low standards. We have simply made different choices in our life up to this point. In an instant someone can go from poor decisions to good decisions. They can change their thinking and therefore change their actions, decisions and choices.

By our values
Strong morals and values are in the minority today. Look at television and movies. They make a mediocre life seem acceptable. They show broken homes and promiscuity as a normal and okay part of life. Television programs have shifted from the ideal family to a life of no responsibility (for anything), lying, cheating, no morals, no value for life and no reverence for God.

Those of us with strong values must stand up and prove this media and worldly shift to be false. Life is too important for us to ignore the basic and pure laws of life.

It is important to understand, I am not saying that if you come from a broken home you are wrong or bad. What I am saying is, let's take responsibility for this life and change everything we can to improve our situation and that of our children. If where you are in life is not where you truly want to be, then take the steps necessary to make the changes needed for improvement. Yes, it may take time and it may be hard, but the reward (getting the life you want) is well worth it.

By our Action… or in-action
As I mentioned earlier, what we do speaks louder than what we say. This especially goes for our impact with children. They are always observing if what we say and what we do match. What a sorry example in life when we tell children they need to be truthful and honest and then they observe us talking about others behind their backs and they hear us tell untruths to "friends". These actions are telling them that everything you said is meaningless. Any future instructions or teachings will be taken with a grain of salt.

An Absolute Lie
Feeling that you are unimportant or insignificant is an absolute lie that cannot be bought into any longer. If you have ridden that train… get off and wake up to the fact that it has been an illusion and a lie.

Every aspect of nature has incredible significance…

>All of nature has:
>>Action
>>Light
>>Power
>>Energy
>>Balance
>>Love
>>and Purpose

Since we are all from Nature we are All of these qualities and much, much more.

Our Purpose is to Love and to Serve

We spoke earlier about having a big enough "why". Our Purpose is to love and to serve, but we get to choose how we want to accomplish this purpose.

The beauty of life is that YOU get to choose "How you Want to Love and Serve the World." Life is Not about being dealt a "hand" and playing the "hand" you are given. Regardless of the circumstances in your life you are *not* stuck. You *can* change your life. God created ALL of us to be amazing and incredible pieces of His bigger plan for Peace.

What is peace?
Peace is expressing Love in True balance. It is important to see EVERY aspect of life as a true and blessed gift. This gift allows you to move along your pathway in life. Peace does not mean no strife or no arguing and no dis-agreeing. There is not only ONE path. Each time we make a choice our path changes. Sometimes the change is slight and sometimes the change is dramatic.

Matthew, our 7 year old, is a great example of peace. He is very confident about what he enjoys in life. He loves to play and have fun. He loves to use his imagination to create pictures, books, games and very elaborate contraptions to make his playtime that much more enjoyable. Matthew has taught me to calmly listen to his latest idea and enjoy the process of me creating it with him. Instead of my former knee jerk reaction of saying "Matt, that is too extravagant" or "There is not time to do that, just play with the toys you already have." He loves making tents, clubhouses, planes out of wood, swords and guns (to get the bad guys). He also enjoys being silly so his brother and sisters laugh. He knows that you cannot laugh and be sad at the same time. One of his goals is to make the world a funnier place. Not to be so serious about everything.

Why may our life not seem blessed?

God has blessed us with the wonderful gift of free will.

> This is where we get to make choices in life.
> What to do or not to do?
> Being honest or dishonest.
> Having integrity or not.
> Doing good or bad.
> Doing right or wrong.

Sometimes when we make choices in life we need to choose hard. It is simple and popular to take the easy way out; however, it is frequently the "hard" choice that leads you to the life you truly desire. This may mean, going against the grain, not doing what everyone else does, just because everyone else is doing it.

God allows us to make these choices and decisions. He loves us through it all; just as we love our *own* children. Even when we make the "wrong" choice God has an amazing way of having us learn and grow from our choices. He still guides us in His desired direction.

The way we know it is God's direction is because things tend to happen in an effortless way, by "coincidence" or by "chance". Dr. Wayne Dyer speaks about the true meaning of coincidence being two angles that fit perfectly together (or co-inside). He uses another word, Synchronous, which also describes this phenomenon very well. Synchronicity is when things are "in sync" or on the same wavelength. They are events that "fall into place" without our conscious thought and planning. There is a definite flow to things when we simply trust and let them happen. So often we get in the way of the flow of life without even realizing it. There is Power in the manifestation process. We do not have to FORCE anything. As a matter of fact, if we try to "force the issue" it actually slows down the Manifestation process. How many times have you been driving in traffic and in a hurry? Every lane you switched to suddenly became the slow lane. Other times you are in the same traffic but you are not in a hurry so you simply go with the flow. You may even let someone into your lane, wave them on and acknowledge their thank you. Amazingly enough, and without a struggle, you get to where you are going without any delays. The more "open control" we have over our day the better it will flow for us. There will be fewer struggles, less wasted time, more productivity and more enjoyment. Most of us have done this in some form already in our lives. The key is to do this every day and consciously.

Whatever You Conceive and Believe You Can Achieve

Write down what IMPACT you would like to have in this world:

_____

_____

_____

_____

_____

_____

What do you feel is your Purpose in life?

_____

_____

_____

_____

_____

_____

_____

What about this purpose is inspiring to you?

Notes

Chapter Six

The Keys To Living an Inspired Life

From Information to Inspiration…The SHIFT Necessary to Live a Life Without Limits! - Dr. G.

When we spoke earlier about STRESS we came to the conclusion that the more we decrease the negative stress in our life the better off we will be. I am very aware that some negative stress is not changeable. Be sure not to be too quick to jump to this conclusion. Many people say, "I do not like my job but there is nothing I can do about it." That is a very untrue statement. One of the main points of *The Ripple Effect* is *consciously creating* your life. This may mean that in the above scenario, this person may have to totally change jobs in order to find decreased stress and greater fulfillment.

Decreasing stress will create a more fulfilling life. Many people state that their highest level of stress comes from a life that is unfulfilling. After spending so many years living according to the world's view, many people have lost sight of God's plan in their life. Breaking this cycle involves shifting from the information age to the inspiration age.

Let me explain what I mean…Information is everywhere!

We have the ability to find out about so many different topics & subjects simply by the click of the mouse.

This is a fantastic innovation…However, what are you doing with this information?

For example…How have you used the information you have already received in this book as well as others that you have read?

Do you read and listen to the information and just forget about it, or do you utilize that information to change your life and the lives of those you love?

How you are utilizing the information in this book is a very good indicator of how you are utilizing anything that is good for you.

If you have been a warrior for life and helped others to learn the principles in this book, you are also typically a person who actually goes to the gym you belong to, takes responsibility for your life, asks questions of your financial advisor to maximize your investing and has a large dedicated circle of friends.

I am not saying that *You* need to save the world…just impact *your* circle of influence.

People who are fulfilled in life are typically healthy and adapt to stress more easily.

No matter what your job or chosen career is, if you are inspired by being involved in it vs. "just having a job to go to day in and day out", you will be much more fulfilled. For some of you it will be obvious what is exciting and fulfilling about what you do every day.

This also goes for stay at home MOMs or DADs. This is one of the most important responsibilities in the world today. You are raising and molding the future.

For some of you, you may have to search for something that is inspiring about what you do.

A simple question to ask is "How does what I do impact the world" or "How does what I do help people." Do not base how important your job is on how much you get paid for what you do. If you have already defined your purpose, then you simply ask, "Is what I am doing now moving me closer to fulfilling my purpose?"

That is a trap of society today. We get so self-centered that we are clueless or care less about what our impact is doing to the rest of the world.

Each of us inspires others, even if it is ONLY by the way we behave, act, and respond each and every day.

I say ONLY, but that –example- is the ONE action that every single one of us does as a service to the world.

A little exercise that could change your life… Find the inspiration in what you do each day. Enjoy this exercise whether it is a Monday or Saturday, a "work"day or a holiday.

See the good.

See the service.

See how you are benefiting.

Once you realize *The Ripple Effect* of *your* life, you will be inspired to take your life to a higher level.

Job and life dissatisfaction is one of the top causes of emotional stress in our lives. Emotional stress is a huge factor in today's society. Earlier we spoke about how the overwhelm of stress causes Subluxations (Nerve Interference), which leads to the future ill health, disease and a low quality of life. As a Chiropractor I correct the area of Subluxation (Nerve Interference) allowing the body to once again heal itself and work the way it was intended. However, we still need to break the cycle of increased stress and life dissatisfaction.

After looking at your day-to-day life, if you just cannot find anything that is inspiring…. It may be time for a career or life change.

People do it all the time and wonder why they waited so long.

My goal for writing this book is to assist you with increasing your Quality of Life.

Do the exercise on the previous page and evaluate your life. Find out how it is inspiring. Expand and upgrade that which is inspiring. This should be exciting everyday regardless of whether you are on vacation, at work, retired or just having FUN.

Let's make everyday fun and inspiring.

Notes

_____

_____

_____

_____

_____

_____

_____

_____

Notes

Chapter Seven

Growth is a Process
This process can feel like a Roller Coaster

*"You Can Not Be In Defense and
Growth At The Same Time."
- Dr. Christopher Kent*

Anything new, like the information in this book, will often make you excited and energized to create change in your life. It is a different way of thinking.

As you begin to make changes, in your personal or professional life, be very aware that this is ALL a process. By definition, a process is something that takes time. You will probably not master all of the strategies and principles the first time you try them.

Many people find that the more times they read this book the better they are able to apply these ideas and incorporating them into their lives.

Begin making changes – determine the one item that resonates with you the most, so far, and experiment with making that small change to your actions and in your thinking.

Take action and enjoy the process of change.

Warning – be very careful when you find changes that are working very well for you. There will often times be people or events that enter your life that will distract you and pull you away from these new changes. Stay strong to resist going back to your "old" ways. If you keep the old actions you get the old results.

When you find changes that are working well for you, do not be satisfied with that as the end result. Look constantly to improve the changes you have made. Strive to make these changes more and more effective in your life.

To this point, you may have never changed anything in your life. You may have always let life happen to you. Now is the time to step up to the microphone and declare what kind of life you want to live.

The bottom line is that change MUST happen in order for growth to occur.

Look at the BUTTERFLY

It goes through an incredible metamorphosis and struggle, but what a beautiful result.

Nature provides us with an endless supply of examples of change, process, struggle, beauty and flow. Have you ever seen a plant that is growing in a crack on the side of a mountain? Did you know that Monarch butterflies fly thousands of miles just to return to the branch they were born on? This is where they reproduce, and the cycle continues.

Keep making the changes.
> Do not make changes for the sake of change, but with real thought, purpose and deliberate action.
> Keep learning more about yourself.
> Keep growing and expanding as a person.

When we stick to the process of change we continue to grow as an individual.

As you continue making changes you will notice a few rules about the process of change.

You will find that it takes TNT:
> **T**ime
> **N**oticeable Dedication
> **T**hought

It is going to take effort to sustain the process of change. Understanding this fact involves understanding these key points:

> Keep making changes.
> Try New ideas.
> Let go of the old that is not working for you.

> Get rid of old thoughts and ideas that no longer serve you.
>
> Look to improve the things you were doing that were okay but not great.

Remember - at any time you can begin anew with a totally clean slate.

YOU MUST keep going or you will drift back to your "old ways".

Overwhelm

Many people get very overwhelmed because they try to make too many changes all at once AND / OR because they have not applied, not to mention mastered, the proper use of Time.

Overwhelm leads to Frustration

You stop doing any of the positive things you already changed.

The rubber band effect goes into full swing and you spring back to doing all the old things that gave you results you do not desire any longer.

Some of the things you changed worked so well that you stop doing them! I know this sounds crazy, but when you look back on the good things that you stopped doing, you have no idea why you ever stopped.

When you get frustrated you then go external. You wonder what are others doing that is working for them? You think to yourself, "I'll just do what they are doing."

Wait – Wait – Wait

DO NOT be a person who simply follows the herd.

Break the Cycle

Do Not Keep Doing the Same Thing!
Respond differently.
Take different action!
Be a leader!
Be a master of your life!
Consciously Create YOUR Life in Your OWN I.D.E.A.L.!

Whenever you look into something new, always remember who you are, so you are sure these great ideas are a fit for you.

The better you know yourself the more you realize everything is not a good fit for you.

You no longer fall into the traps of society. These traps are: Doing what others do just to not feel like an "outsider". Caring about what others think. Not being true to who you really are.

BEWARE whenever you start to Revert back to the "old" ways!

DO NOT doubt the process.

If you slip and begin to do "old" things again…

Do not beat yourself up.

Remember you ALWAYS have the tool of a Clean Slate. Simply wipe it clean, learn and begin anew.

People are always slipping when it comes to diets and exercise programs. That is okay. Learn from what we have done in the past and change in order to take a, consciously chosen, different path next time.

Most people in the world do not have control of their time or their finances. This is why these are two of the most important Mastery Systems that I discuss when I Coach others, give seminars or write Books.

Mastery of the Process of Change

What it takes to master the process of change is simply having the knowledge that it will take time and there will be distractions.

The more you can keep focused on the present and the process - the more effortless it will all be for you. You will have periods of major breakthroughs as you continue to master time and money – and as you learn to master the idea of Service as well.

Dr. Thomas Edward Gargiula

Notes

Notes

Chapter Eight

Drawing a Line In The Sand
What Used To Be Acceptable No Longer Exists

*"If you don't stand for something
you WILL fall for everything"* - Anonymous

One of the underlying premises of *The Ripple Effect* is to create and design your OWN Ideal Life.

This allows you to consciously create your life for you and for anyone else who you invite into your life.
We have discussed in previous chapters, the topic of True Wealth.

> We discussed that True Wealth is not only about money but also about living a life that we enjoy, cherish and consciously create.
>
> This is where *Drawing A Line In The Sand* comes into play.

On one side of *The Line* is that area where everything ideal in your life resides. The other side of the line is where the things that are no longer ideal live.

Ideal things might be:
    Choice of career
    Choice of spouse
    Your Children
    Whatever else is ideal

Let's take a moment to define what we mean by IDEAL

Something Ideal is very personal.

What is Ideal for you?

What works for you?

Earlier in the book I suggest what I.D.E.A.L. represents.

I.D.E.A.L.:

  I : To live a life that has positive IMPACT
  D: To live with DIVINITY
  E: To live life EFFORTLESSLY
  A: To be ATTRACTIVE – Love Yourself
  L: To Always come from a position of LOVE

    NOW we have to go back to what you really like, what you want in life and how you choose to create your life. It ALWAYS comes back to *you* deciding what *you* really want in life.

It is not what works for someone else, regardless of how much respect we may have for that person.

We have to begin making decisions and choices based upon what *we want* and NOT based upon what others will think of us.

A few classic examples:

If I buy an expensive car and drive it around town, what will other people think?

Will they think I'm shoving the fact that I have been diligent with accumulating some money in their face?

If we move to a bigger house or buy expensive toys will our "friends" think we believe we are better than them?

After all... I do not want to hurt anyone else's feelings.

I do not want to rock the boat.

Will my parents think I am being frivolous?

If I work less than 5 days per week will other

people think I am lazy or unsuccessful or gaining my money in a devious way in order to take days off?

What will my parents / siblings say?

WHO CARES WHAT OTHER PEOPLE THINK?!

Notes

_____
_____
_____
_____
_____
_____
_____
_____
_____
_____
_____
_____
_____

Chapter Nine

Who Cares What Other People Think?

"What you think of me is none of my business."

This is why it is so difficult for us to come up with our life plan the first time we do it. We put a bunch of other people's stuff into it.

Once we go through the process a few times and we evolve as a person, we are amazed at the results.

Most of us see that, even though the money is awesome, it is not only about the money.

It is about enjoying life and doing it for the right reasons.

SO WHAT IS ENJOYABLE TO YOU!
    First you
    Then your spouse
    Then your children

By going through this process on a monthly basis you really get to create a pretty neat life – THIS BECOMES YOUR FUEL FOR GROWTH.

The number one answer I hear from people when I ask them what motivates them is… "I don't know!"

HAVING A CONSCIOUSLY CREATED LIFE PLAN WILL LEAD TO A GROWING BUSINESS AND AN EVER EXPANDING LIFE!

The more Crystal Clear you become about what is ideal for you, the less tolerant you are about things that do not come up to your ideal standard.

We MUST set our own Standards and Boundaries.

Standards and boundaries are your *minimal acceptable guidelines* for people, events, circumstances, finances and relationships in your life.

This is different than expectations

> We also spoke about expectations, by living life without expectations of others, it is very freeing. That does not mean people can walk all over our standards and boundaries. It means that if they want to play in our "game called life" their actions must meet our standards.

> By NOT having expectations, it means you are not bothered by who does and who does not choose to play in your life and by your rules! This thought process is not geared toward excluding people. Anyone can choose to raise their standards to meet yours.

Let me give a simple example of why this is not an elitist attitude. It is one of my standards and boundaries not to be around people who choose to use foul language. If I happen to end up in someone's company who begins to use foul language I will let them know that I am offended by that and either they will stop or I will remove myself from the situation. I am not saying I am better than them. I have no desire to compare myself with anyone else. I do have to be true to myself and stick to my standards and boundaries.

The more crystal clear we get the pickier we become about:

> our clients
> our friends
> all relationships
> our children's behavior
> our financial arrangements

When we pass the tests that will invariably happen, to test how serious we are about our standards and boundaries, there will be an amazing change in:

> our clients
> our friends
> all relationships
> our children's behavior
> our financial arrangements

The quality of the relationships will increase and your life will begin to become effortless. By effortless I do not mean easy. I mean that life will develop a certain flow.

HOWEVER…

We keep getting tested by things from the unacceptable side.

Example:
> Business volume goes down, temporarily, and we start thinking about lowering our minimally acceptable guidelines to include anyone with a pulse and any type of payment.
>
> Constantly be evaluating your acceptables, keep expanding what is ideal to you AND *stay the course!*
>
> You must continue to expand what you want to *Dump* from your life, what part of your life you want to *Upgrade*, and what parts of your life are now considered *Unacceptable*.

NOW THE BIG TEST

Relationships that do not meet your minimally acceptable guidelines.
    Clients
    Staff – Team Members
    Friends
    Family members

If the concern is in a Serious Relationship, Do Not just blow through it and dump it. First ask, "Is this a relationship that is upgradeable?"

Many times, because of our "example", the people we care the most about will also begin changing on their own or asking us what we are doing so they can improve their lives as well.

Upgrade what is truly worth upgrading and be okay with Dumping the rest.

When you dump a, Client, Team Member, Friendship, or Unhealthy financial arrangement, you grow to new heights. It is like you are a hot air balloon that just let go of huge sand bags weighing it down. Sometimes it can be a little scary, but enjoy the ride!

Notes

Chapter Ten

Upgrading The Quality of Your Life
Because The "Old" Way Is No Longer Okay

*"You Can Not Get To A New Port
Unless You Leave The Harbor"*

The core purpose of *The Ripple Effect* is to help you increase the Quality of your life.

What exactly do I mean by this?

Well, if you have a barrier in any area of your life, the removal of that barrier will help improve your current situation, and it will advance your thinking as well as your total growth process. It is just like driving a car with the emergency brake still applied. I know, I am the only one who has ever done that. (Ha,Ha) I have done that both literally and figuratively. For those of you who have never done this, let me explain. You are driving your car, pushing the gas pedal, the car goes but there is an obvious force holding the car back. You look around with surprise and wonderment, until you discover that the emergency brake is still on. You put a big smile on your face, release the brake, and it feels so good to be driving so freely and effortlessly.

When we make improvements (removing the emergency brake) to our life, even simple ones, they will often times lead to an incredible cascading of other positive changes.

It does take purposeful action to find and remove these barriers so improvements can be made in your life. You cannot just wish barriers to be gone and think they should disappear simply because you are a nice person. We must take responsibility and take action.

When you feel better about your life, you will sleep better –

That leads to increased energy–

Increased energy causes an improvement in your performance at work –

This improved performance, over time, leads to a raise, bonus, promotion, or a larger opportunity for your future.

You will be attracting other people into your life to support your new attitude.

You see, it is very important to understand that your life is a direct reflection of who you are.

It is pretty amazing what can happen when we are in control of our thoughts.

Everything we experience will have an impact upon our lives and the lives of the people around us.

Here is what I mean...

> If we feel better, have more energy and perform better at work, we become happier with ourselves. Eventually our happiness becomes a state of mind and not the result of having a good or bad day.
>
> The significance of this is huge – because – it is when we are down on ourselves that we tend to take it out on the ones we love the most...
>
> When we choose to be happy with ourselves we open up to enjoying other people and other situations.
>
> So, by being happy with ourselves and having more balance in our life, we treat others in a much nicer way.
>
> When we are nice to others, this adds to their feelings of self-esteem, and they pass on this niceness to others.

Before you know it you have directly and indirectly impacted the lives of thousands of people in the course of just one day.

Multiply this by weeks, months and years and you have just impacted the lives of hundreds of thousands of people.

As I have stated earlier… "IF we will have an impact" is no longer the question.

The question now becomes…

What kind of an impact do I choose to have on this world?

The impact can be...

> Good or Bad
> Positive or Negative
> Love or Hate
> Peace or Conflict
> The choice is yours… and the resulting consequences of that choice are also yours.

Think of how it would feel living in those two different worlds.

> One world of Good or One World of Bad
> One of Positive or One of Negative
> One of Love or One of Hate
> One of Peace or One of War

Think of how living in these two different worlds would impact your…

 Health
 Enjoyment
 Freedoms
 Finances
 Opportunities

When living in a scenario based on evil, negativity, hatred & strife…

You have a much higher level of stress. It is more difficult to adapt to such stresses.

The result is the presence of subluxation…

 Nerve interference
 Breakdown
 Poor health
 Disease
 Symptoms
 A low quality of life and
 Often – an early death

What would the opposite world look like?

Two people can look at the world and see two totally different situations:

 One sees Good…the other sees Bad.
 One Positive…the other Negative.

One enjoys a life filled with Love…the other Hate. One sees Peace…the other sees War.

It is all about perspective.

I am not suggesting ignoring the world and being ignorant to what exists out there - however - we attract what we give off and we attract what we focus on.

I know – you may be thinking that you focus on love, peace, health, increased business and better finances - and you still get the bottom of the barrel.

In order for these natural laws to work *we must be living a life of balance and integrity.*

The reason why I say integrity is because we often love externally, are good to others, care about others… which is great – BUT…

We totally ignore the internal.

We do not show ourselves love, respect, caring and a positive attitude.

In many cases – if someone else treated us like we treat ourselves, we would disown him or her as an acquaintance – much less a real friend.

Let's look inside for a minute.

Let's be self-full for a minute.

Not selfish…self-full.

Let's love ourselves enough to show ourselves the respect, the caring and a the positive attitude – that anyone deserves.

No one will give you love, caring, and respect if you don't give it to yourself first.

Let's face it – God made you out of love!

Years ago there was a kid's T-shirt that said, "God Doesn't Make Junk."

It was created to remind people that children are people too; they count for a whole lot and they are our future.

Being self-full has a great positive Ripple Effect.

If we respect ourselves we will NOT treat our bodies like JUNK! (This is where most people's biggest contradiction lies!)

We will love ourselves and care enough that we will start making healthy choices for our body and our life.

> We will feed our body healthier food.
> We will exercise our body.
> We will change from "bad" or unhealthy habits to "good" or healthy ones – such as stopping smoking, excess drinking, drugs, etc.

Before we know it we begin getting healthier. But even more happens than "just" that.

Positive things begin to happen to us.

Nice friendships come along naturally.

Unhealthy relationships either get upgraded or vanish completely.

Work either becomes enjoyable or a better opportunity comes along.

Why and How does this happen?
We begin to, unconsciously, demand respect and we are also giving others incredible levels of respect, love, peace and kindness.

Since we have the conscious choice over how we view life, how we treat ourselves and the benefits of that choice… why would anyone choose anything but taking impeccable care of themselves?

Well…There are a couple of reasons.

The first reason for someone not taking great care of them self is because many people do not know that they have any control over any aspect of their life.

Think about it…

If they acknowledged that they had any power over

their current state or situation, then they would have to take *responsibility* for their "lot" in life.

You see, if you do not acknowledge it you cannot change it.

Do not beat yourself up over the past.

Just know that you can change the future if you want to. Start with a clean slate, find your purpose, and then take action steps that will lead in the direction of the fulfillment of your purpose. By having a clearly defined purpose, as we discussed earlier, it is easier to stay on task and to have fewer distractions. If you are taking a trip from New York to Los Angeles, and you have the directions and the roadmap, it is easier to stay on course. There are many attractions to see along the way to Los Angeles, but if the goal is to get to Los Angeles in the most efficient manner possible, then it is easier to ignore distractions. If the goal is to get to Los Angeles eventually while enjoying each and every aspect of this beautiful country, then detours are welcomed and no longer distractions. The detours are built in as part of the program.

I suggest that by having a life purpose, we are able to follow the roadmap to its logical and planned conclusion.

However, we also need to be open to the flow of God's plan. Remember what we spoke about in Chapter 2. The more in communication we are with God, through prayer, meditation, reading His word, and Eucharist, the more our plan and God's plan will begin to look alike.

The second reason for not taking great care of your self is because no one has ever given them permission to enjoy life. No one has shared with you that it is okay if you live life to the fullest. No one mentioned how great it is when you view the glass as half full instead of half empty. People forgot to tell you it is absolutely alright to see the positive in anything instead of focusing on the negative in everything. It is important to see the balance and to honor the difference. After all what seems like a down turn may simply be what is needed to gather momentum to reach your next big goal.

So – not that you should need it, but if you do, I am right now giving you the permission to create the life of your dreams.

You see, by living the life of your dreams, that inspired life we spoke about in earlier chapters, you get to not only have a great life, but you also get to help a lot of people along the way to "Increase the quality of their life"!

Notes

Notes

Chapter Eleven

KNOWING That You Are Creating/ Living Your I.D.E.A.L. Life

"The Joys of Life, Success, Serving, and Victory is not in the destination, but in the Journey" – Dr. G.

In this world of noise and chaos it is important to take the time to step away from the bombardment of input and to step into the silence of your mind.

It is by being silent that allows our heart to hear.

Have you ever asked yourself these questions or gone through this thought process?

> Am I doing what God wants me to do?
> Am I doing all that I am supposed to be doing?
> Is there more for me to do or am I okay being where I am, and should I stay here?

> How do I know if it is my life I am living?
> I am enjoying my life…do I have to push it to a higher level?

I am a firm believer that the more well defined you have your values, standards & boundaries and your vision for your life, then things will develop in an effortless way.

However you cannot simply define your life once and forget about it. If you have ever done that, it is easy to lose your passion and your drive. Every day you need to reset your thought process. The more you do this the more difficult it will be to slip away from this habit and life building strategy.

Many of us have done this in the past with our exercise and our nutritional lifestyle. We enjoy the benefits of exercise and good eating and at the time we think it would be crazy to ever stop this good process. HOWEVER, life happens and things get in the way of the good process and habits. Slowly, poor habits and poor lifestyle choices begin to insidiously enter your life. Before you know it you have lost energy, gained weight and found all sources of motivation and positive drive having waned.

Why do you think that is?

Many times it is because your life was not well defined.

What are your core values?

What is the role of finances in your life?

What is the role of your relationships?

What are your standards & boundaries for both Business & Personal relationships?

The more spelled out your life is and the more detail you go into, the freer you feel to just let life flow. Then what shows up is your ideal life.

Keep a List of Blessings and keep a journal.

Each day/week keep a list of the things you are thankful for. Business, professional, personal, family, friends, etc.

This is your personal Testimonial Book.

You cannot read this list without realizing how incredibly blessed you are in this life.

The journal is a wonderful tool to document your life. Putting your thoughts, feelings and events on paper (or into a computer) will allow you to expand your mind, open your heart and have a far greater impact on this beautiful world of ours.

What type of impact do you intend to have upon this world?

Everyone has an impact… you simply need to decide what type of impact you intend on having.

Strategies for having a positive impact!

The Gratitude Principle

You must first have gratitude and love for yourself and have that spill over onto others from the abundance or excess that you share in your heart.

Anything we give away or share should come from our abundance.

Do you know anyone who gives from their abundance of guilt, hatred, negativity and victim choices? There are plenty of people like this in the world and possibly in your own life.

What a joy when we meet people who give from their abundance of ... Love, Energy, Time, & Money

Love
Guard your heart – but LOVE everyone. It sounds like a strange thought. Think about it. Jesus commands us to Love our "neighbor" as ourselves. Right there is the problem for some of us. We do not love ourselves that much so we do the same to our "neighbor". This is why I said we must love ourselves so much that it simply spills over onto everyone else. Do not discriminate who you love. Your heart is your true core essence. Let people into your heart who are giving, loving and caring. After all, with enough love, anyone can be giving, loving, and caring.

Energy

Guard your energy. It is very easy to have it drained from you. There are people (the ones who only focus on the negative side of everything) who are happy to drain your energy because they think it will actually increase their energy.

You can visually protect your-self with a shield of white light. Visualize your body surrounded with white light. Picture a halo that covers your whole body. This acts as a filter. This allows you to share your energy with everyone, but it cannot be sucked from you.

Your Energy is your life force. It is a blessing and a gift from God. Guard it well.

Time (Dynamic Time Structure)

You first must master your time.

Then choose to give some of it away, in the form of volunteering, helping friends or family, etc. Like Health and Wealth, Time is such a complex subject; it will be covered in depth in "The Ripple Effect of Time Mastery"

Money

First get your own finances straightened out and have a plan for your life (consciously created, of course) then choose to give money to whatever organizations, charities, churches, and foundations you decide to support.

There should be No Guilt attached to the giving.

Do it Simply out of pure love.

Clean Slate
This is all about forgiving your-"self" and starting over. You can use a Clean Slate anytime you want and as often as you want.

Just because you never gave from your abundance before does not mean you cannot begin now!!!

It is being self-full to take care of your own stuff first. You must first fill your own personal needs. This is very important because if you do not fill yourself up first then anything you do or give to another will be depleting your valuable supply of whatever you are giving. When we do this often we then fully deplete our supply and have nothing left for future giving.

It is not being selfish. Being selfish means Never giving anything that you have to another.

Being self-full is taking care of things from the inside out. This is a very natural way of doing things. Look at a river. It supplies the surrounding area with moisture and water from its abundance. If a river's source is cut off, and it continues to give, then it will drain itself of water, dry up and never be able to supply life-giving water ever again. The result is - the surrounding plants and animals will die or have to move on to the next supply of water.

Think about the importance of giving from your abundance. If you drain your own supplies you will only be able to do for others for a short period of time. However, when you come from your abundance you can be of service for a lifetime.

If you are not taking care of your life from the Inside-Out then you are doing it from the Outside-In and that is the opposite of Natural Law.

Since God created nature and all of the natural laws and processes, going against nature is doing things against God.

Doing things this way becomes very effortful. You tend to have to force things. Life tends to always seem the same. Nothing ever changes.

An example of this would be if your business or life would grow for a little bit then spring back to where it was before. This is a good indication that we are not passing some test that is being asked of us. Sometimes this is very subtle, but it always stands true.

You may have tried to change certain habit patterns. Something always happens and the old patterns return.

You may have:

>Started smoking again.
>Stopped working out.

Stopped being conscious about the food you eat.
Stopped getting the proper amount of sleep each night.

You MUST be okay with this. We are not going for perfection here. Remember The Clean Slate process. This is a great tool that gives you a do-over with NO guilt attached.

Here is one of the main reasons why we repeat old behaviors that we do not want to repeat. Our Thoughts lead to specific Feelings which lead to Actions which give us very Specific Results. Many people want a different result so they change the action steps. They will get a different result but it seems to only be temporary. WHY?!?

You have to go all the way back and change the thought process that started this whole cascade. You see, a good friend of mine, Dr. David Jackson, says, "People act on their beliefs whether they are aware of their beliefs or not and whether their beliefs are true or not!!!"

Translated – We MUST first change the Thoughts in our mind, and then the feelings will be different. A change in our feelings will lead to different actions and then different and long lasting results.

Being Silent in the midst of a chaotic world!

This allows you to be happy and content with where you are in life. Taking a break for balance and to clear your mind gives you an opportunity to re-focus.

By doing this you can be silent in the middle of any situation where it seems chaotic, noisy and out of balance.

It is all about consciously creating our life in our own I.D.E.A.L..

You have ALWAYS Created your own life. Most of us have not taken responsibility for this fact. You have the choice to create your life the way *you* want it or to let someone else create it for you!!!

After all – we created where we are right now. Our life is a direct reflection of who we are. We did it months and years ago through our actions and inactions.

Remember – "If it could have been, it would be that way". The actions that you have taken have directly resulted in where you are right now.

Why not take control and consciously create it for yourself. Do it as an experiment… see if you like the NEW life. The New You. You can always go back to the old way!

"Am I Refusing to be less than I can be so I don't show up others who refuse to be ALL that they can be?"

This is often what is holding us back. This is such a great question. It has everything to do with not playing small.

Nelson Mandela stated, "Who are *you* not to show your greatness." After all you are a piece of God. How dare you not use your gifts and your talents? I mentioned in the beginning of this book... "Your life is God's gift to you, so how you live it and what you do with this gift is your gift right back to God. Do NOT short change God. You are such an incredible person.

The above quote describes the trap so many of us have fallen into over the years. We do not want to show up others because, after all, what would they think if we did succeed and did become successful?

You know what? I have said it before, but it bears repeating many times. WHO CARES WHAT THEY THINK! Stop focusing on the world and what "it" thinks about you and start focusing on what condition you want to leave this world in, and where you want to spend eternity. This is very straight-forward because it is that simple. When we are clear in our thinking and with our purpose, the answers are very simple. They may not be easy, but they will be simple.

Our responsibility is to create a great life that we enjoy, and to serve others to our highest ability possible. *Our responsibility is not about being small in order to make other small thinkers happy and feel good about their small choices in life.*

Remember, our life is *our* responsibility. It is not about the need to make more money or to get another award. It is about having a wonderful, eternal and positive Impact upon this world.

Notes

Notes

Chapter Twelve

Working on the BEING instead of the DOING

"You act according to your belief, whether that belief is true or not, and even if you are unaware of your deepest belief."
- Dr. David Jackson

How many of us, in the past, have wanted this year to be different than last year, but we do not take any different action and then are surprised when this year turns out exactly the same as last year – or possibly worse.

The actions we take come from our thinking. So what we need to do is work on our being. Work on our Thought-fullness. As we work on our thinking, our beliefs, what we need to do begins to change automatically and sometimes even effortlessly.

It is not only about *doing* things differently, it is about *being* (Thinking) different.

Here is where the focus needs to shift: It is Not only what you DO. You must focus on who you *are* as a person.

I know many people get frustrated with that statement. I have several Professional Coaching clients who think they only need to DO differently, but once they learn about the Being aspect of things, and give it a chance, they see the power in BEING (thinking) different.

I do not mean to say that "doing" is not important. Many of us have experienced, either through ourselves or through a friend, where things were done differently but the results were the same. This often leads to frustration.

The reason why the new or altered action did not bring about a different result is because the person taking the different action has not changed.

We see the same scenario in many other aspects of our own life.

Think about it… Why do you go to the restaurants, theater, musical or play… why do you go to the baseball, football or hockey stadium to see a game when you can watch it in the comfort of your own home with a better vantage point of the event and a better climate?

Is it because of a promotion, a gift certificate or sale that is going on? Or is it because of the experience that you receive when there. The experience is the BEING.

So, how do you want to change the Experience of your life? The way you experience life is your "Being-ness".

Another part of living that brings out our "Being-ness" is the INTENT of why we do what we do in our lives.

Why are you immediately attracted to some people and repelled by others? – It cannot be their DOING or actions because they have not done anything besides shared their BEING-ness with you.

The attraction is the BEING not the DOING. It is the energy that you feel from that person or from a situation. We have all experienced when a situation or a person does not "FEEL" right to us. When we listen to this inner voice we are always better off. We frequently see an immediate reason why it was good that we listened to our inner voice.

The more we are focused on our being the louder the inner voice becomes. It is like tuning into the correct radio station. The message becomes crystal clear. There is no confusion as to what the message is asking us to do. This is listening to your heart.

When we feel an attraction toward another person or event it is the experience of being in the presence of your BEING. When this attraction is for another person it is not only meant as a physical attraction, like with a spouse. (When it is your spouse the attraction is on many levels.)

However, I am also speaking of the platonic attraction for a friend or even a business partner. The attraction I am discussing goes beyond the physical realm of attraction and onto spirit to spirit and soul to soul.

Since it is that powerful, do you think it would be of value to work on our BEING?

For those of you who are still thinking, NO I do not want to work on my "Being", just give me something to do and, like a "good" student, I will do it. Life and our humanness is not a mechanical project that connects Point A to Point B. – If this is your thought try this:

Please view this as an experiment.

If after doing this "working on your Being" as an experiment, you do not like how you feel or the results you get, you can always go back to what you have always done and get those same results.

SO… there is nothing to lose – give it a try!!!

How do we make our BEING attractive?

We increase the attractiveness of our BEING-ness in two ways.

Number one
Have a Balanced life!

How to become balanced in our life!

There are several areas of our lives that can be broken down into categories.

Physical Health
    Am I happy with how I feel?
    Do I have any health concerns?
    Do I like the way I look?
    Do I like the way I feel in my clothes?
    Have I had my teeth, eyes, hearing, blood, and Nervous System checked lately?

Spiritual Health
    Do I feel connected to God?
    Have I really accepted Jesus Christ as my Savior?
    Do I communicate daily with God through prayer and reading?
    Do I take the time to listen to God – Daily?
    Have I received true forgiveness for ALL of my sins?
    Do I have an accountability partner? This is someone who will give you love, support, and challenge. They will help you become the person you want to be. This person will not let you slip back to the old you.

Mental Health
    Do I feel my life is out of control?

Do I take time for me?
Do I challenge and expand my thinking on a regular basis?

Social Health
Do I spend time regularly with friends?
Have I made a new friend in the past year?
Do I serve my community on some level?

Family Health
Do I spend time with my family regularly?
Am I on good terms with my family members?
Have I come to peace with and forgiven any and all past family issues?
Do I make time for family because they are such a high priority in my life?

Financial Health
Do I know where I really am financially?
Do I spend more than I make?
Do I have a plan?
Do I follow the plan?

Career Health
Do you enjoy what you do?
Is what you do fulfilling your Life's Purpose?
If you did not need the money, would you still do what you are doing?

Grade each category on a scale of 1 to 10 (with 10 as great and 1 as poor)

Be totally honest with yourself and not too hard on yourself as well. You see people respond two different ways to this type of an evaluation. They either falsely state that everything is great and do not look at their life in an honest and true way, or they are overly hard on themselves and give themselves an untrue low score.

This is a very private look at your life. Feel free to share it with others or with no one at all.

First Thought

If you need assistance with your score ask your spouse or a close friend. Both of you should do the evaluation and see where the answers are the same and where they differ.

A spouse or close friend will be able to guide you to a more accurate score.

If you are the type of a person who is hard on yourself they will be able to point out where these scores should be higher and give you good reasons why.

Many people view what they do in life as "no big deal". Yet if someone else did the same thing they would be the first to say how great or wonderful the act of giving, loving or service was.

If you are of the personality who says everything is great regardless of the truth, your spouse or friend can gently bring you back to earth and assist you with a more accurate score.

Second Thought

If you presently do not have a specific "Career" due to retirement or because you are a stay-at-home Mom or Dad, then look at this category this way...

Substitute Career Health for that which motivates and inspires you to serve.

It may be:
- Volunteering
- Church
- Teaching your children
- A Charitable Foundation
- Being an awesome example of Love in society.

This list can be endless, but you must identify what you want this category to mean for you. – And it is okay for this to change over the years.

I recommend doing this *Balance Exercise* every three months.

Number Two

GETTING YOUR NEEDS MET outside of your "job" and personal life.

What do I mean?

First you have to figure out what your needs are!

Everyone has different needs

Common needs
The Need for Accomplishment
The Need of being Praised
The Need to be Loved
The Need to be right
The Need for feeling that you Have Value
The Need to feel like you are the "Captain" of your ship

What you need to figure out is
What are your needs?
How do you know what your needs are? Evaluate your life – what do you seek from other people, other relationships and events.

Do you constantly put yourself in situations where you are needed – everything relies on you – do you ever create upset just so you have something to fix?

I know that creating a problem just so you feel needed to fix the problem sounds crazy, but think about it. It is easy to get bored when things are going smoothly. We may self-sabotage a situation because of our need. It is very important to know what your needs are and how to get them met in a healthy way. This will prevent self-sabotaging the seven categories of life that you graded earlier. (You did take the time to grade your life, didn't you?) – Remember you are extremely worth it.

Take the time to do it now if you skipped it the first time.

My Personal System for Meeting My Needs in My Personal Life
Automatic Needs Satisfaction System

Needs That I Have That Need To Be Met
    Accomplishment
    Balance
    Having Value
    Love
    Being the "Captain" of my ship

The things to do to meet my needs in my personal life
    Accomplishment:
    Reading
    Exercising
    Praying / Meditating

Balance
    In Bed by 11PM
    Up at 5:30AM – get focused on my purpose
    Read for 30 minutes in PM
    Exercise 4 times per week
    Pray / Meditate (AM & PM)
    One Day per week for me
      Get into nature
      Time to think, Create, Be at peace

Having Value
    Acknowledging the Valuable things I do have.
    My Family, Friends
    Having a Purpose
    Health, Abundance, Prosperity

Love
    Fill myself with Love.
    First LOVE myself.
    Love everyone.
    Do this through action with NO expectations.
    Do acts of kindness just to do them.

Being the "Captain" of my Ship
    By Doing the above steps.

Notes

_____

_____

_____

_____

_____

_____

_____

_____

Notes

Chapter Thirteen

The Ripple Effect of Time Mastery

"People will value your time when you value your time" – Dr. G.

When I ask people, "What causes the most stress in your life?" the most common answer I hear is, "I have NO time!" "There is so much to do and NO time to do it." Time is a commodity that, at first look, appears to be limited. There are only 24 hours in a day and only 365 days in a year.

Why is it that certain people seem more productive than others? We have all heard the saying, "If you want something done, give it to a busy person."

If we are all given the gift of the same number of hours in a day, how is it that this productivity difference exists? The key difference is the use of the time. Is our time used efficiently or is it wasted? What are we really doing with those hours?

To be sure there is understanding with what I am saying; I am talking about being productive, not about being a work-a-holic. This is a great time to re-visit the basic premise of *The Ripple Effect*.

The Ripple Effect has a basic premise of Consciously Creating MY Life in MY Own I.D.E.A.L.

I.D.E.A.L. has a deeper meaning that expands the major premise of *The Ripple Effect*.

- I : Live your life with INTEGRITY
- D: Live your life with DIVINITY
- E: Live your life with EXCELLENCE
- A: Live your life from a position of being ATTRACTIVE
- L: Live your life with a mantra of LOVE

This Major Premise is wrapped up in Self-Full Love. We must first be grateful to God for making us in His image. We must love ourselves as we love God. Our love needs to be full to overflowing. This overflow is what spills onto everyone else in our life.

Think about it this way. When you are on an airplane and they are going over the safety instructions they say, "In case there is a loss in cabin pressure, there are oxygen masks that will drop down from overhead. If you are seated with a child, FIRST put your mask on so you can BETTER assist your child."

WOW - How simple, yet how profound.

How many times have we run around helping everyone else put on their "oxygen masks" and because we did not take care of our own mask FIRST, we cause harm to ourselves. Harm like, getting sick, not getting our own very important stuff done, neglecting our other responsibilities, procrastinated something that does need to get done, missed an opportunity for personal or professional growth. When we cause harm to ourselves, now who can we help...Nobody. We are useless to others and we are done. Now we are unable to help others, even if we want to and like to. We have made the situation much worse. We are not only helpless, but now others need to help us. They are helping us because we neglected to take care of ourselves in the first place.

As a Wellness Chiropractor and Success Coach, I see the same thing all of the time. People neglect their own health because "there is no time" and because "I have so much on my plate already". It is critical to understand that treating ourselves like this goes against God's Laws and the Principles of Nature. Anytime we go against God's Laws and Natural Principles something eventually breaks down. All it takes is time to see that living this way will not continue without a problem developing.

The most important thing that allows us to have the impact that we feel we are called to, is through Time Mastery. As we Master our Time we are able to accomplish more and do so in a more efficient manner.

The first step in Time Mastery is deciding what your Core Values are. This is how you decide what is important to you and where things fall as a priority in your life. As an example I will share my Core Values with you.

Dr. G.'s Core Values
    God
    Family
    Me
    Sue
    Children
    Service
    Prosperity
    Freedom

Everyone's Core Values are different. You need to decide what is important to you. Once you have your list and order of Core Values you never say "Yes" to something that does not pass each Core Value as a filter. If something passes each Core Value then it is on the table to say "Yes" or not. A simple, but common example is when we say "Yes" to something that interferes with our family time or our time for ourselves.

I have ME as the first thing on the family list. Remember, this is not a selfish move; it is all about putting on my oxygen mask first. After that, for me, it is all about serving others, beginning with my wife and children.

Once you have your Core Values in place you then decide how much time each week you want to spend doing the things you do. All of the things that you do in the course of your week can fall into one of three categories.

Time Categories
    Fun Time
    Productive Time
    Neutral Time

Schedule Fun Time first. There will never be time for fun if you schedule it last or only do fun things when the extra time shows up. Fun is so important for you and for your relationship with your spouse, children, and friends. Fun adds an incredible spice to life. By scheduling fun things first it lets you and your loved ones know that they are valued. You will be amazed at how good this feels. You are getting your needs met. Your family is getting their needs met. The result of this is fulfillment, enjoyment, and love. These results are what is most often missing that causes families and marriages to drift apart. Schedule FUN FIRST!!!

Productive time: This is the time that results in your financial prosperity. This is the time that the farmer spends sowing and tending the fields so the harvest will get reaped. Remember the saying you heard many times as a child. "You reap what you sow." Productive time is very valuable and needs to not be interrupted except for very specific emergencies. Be sure that your loved ones and your colleagues know the importance of this time. You are able to accomplish so much when we are not disturbed or distracted. Do not fool yourself to thinking that all of your "work" hours are productive. As a matter of fact, if you have control over your hours and schedule, the more productive time you put in during a week, the fewer hours you have to spend "working". Productive time is for those things that only you can do and that you do best. For example, I am a Wellness Chiropractor. What I love to do in my office the most is work with practice members through adjusting their Nerve System. There are many other tasks to do. The phones need to be answered, the schedules are kept up to date, money is collected, missed appointments are called, etc. All of these types of tasks are delegated to my awesome team members. This frees me up to enjoy 20 hours of adjusting practice members and 10 hours of productive time to write. A lot gets accomplished and I still have a tone of time to spend with the family.

Neutral Time: This is the time when you do the things that are not super productive. Many of these things you will delegate. Some, however still need to get done. Many of the neutral activities tend to be house related. Cleaning, yard work, grocery shopping, repairs, upgrades, etc. I know what you are thinking... most of the things I just listed can also be delegated. You are 100% correct. You get to decide how much of your neutral time activities you want to delegate. This will free up even more time. If you are thinking about the cost of delegating all of the activities, think about this. If it takes you 5 hours per week to do the neutral time activities, you may be able to add 1 or 2 productive hours per week and have that pay for all of the delegating. You just bought yourself 3 - 4 more hours of fun time. Kind of a neat concept.

Your time is up to you. I consider my time of Earth as a gift and I want to make sure I am using that time wisely and giving back in service as well. Start with the simple exercise of keeping track of every hour of your time for a week. Break down your days into hours for 7 days and as you are going through your day keep track of where you are, what you are doing, and if it is Fun, Productive, or Neutral. Add up the results and see how you can improve your Time Mastery.

Remember - Enjoy the Process!

Notes

Conclusion

There is no Them – There is only US

We are ALL made in the image and likeness of God. God is our one true source. This is the same regardless of whom we are speaking about. Our neighbor – from God, our boss – from God, the homeless person – from God, people who are very old or very young – from God, people in another country regardless of race, color or creed – from God. Even people who do things that are horrible – from God.

Our focus needs to shift from what the person does or what they look like to who the person is and where they come from.

This holds a huge level of importance because so many people go through their day making fun of, gossiping about, being mean to, being prejudiced against and simply dismissing other individuals on the basis that THEY are different from US.

There is NO THEY. We are all the same. We need to remember to think of others for who they are spiritually. Our focus should shift to treating others and loving others for who they are, truly.

The more we live our life from inspiration, focusing on the law of attraction and being aware of the impact that we have upon other's lives, the easier it becomes to treat others with love and respect.

Find your true passion in life. See how this passion leads to your Life's Purpose. Focus on attracting opportunities into your life that will fulfill your Purpose. The more we get out of our own way, let our will match God's will, then things begin to flow. Remember "Thy WILL be done!"

Always remember to enjoy this great and beautiful journey you are on. At each step of the way there is love and beauty to enjoy.

Thank you for choosing to have a wonderful impact upon this world.

All My Love & Appreciation,

Dr. G.

Contact Dr. Tom Gargiula for further information, additional copies of *The Ripple Effect,* or for Speaking Engagements eMail:

DrG@TheRippleEffectLife.com
or Call 314-708-4120

For more information on *The Ripple Effect* and its topics visit: www. TheRippleEffectLife.com.

Sign up as a free member to receive continued information, insight and support on your journey.

God Bless You!

Made in the USA
Middletown, DE
26 June 2015